IMAGES OF WAR

THE BATTLE OF BRITAIN

IMAGES OF
WAR

THE BATTLE OF BRITAIN

Maureen Hill

Photographs by the

Daily Mail

p

Introduction

By so many to so few

'Never in the field of human conflict was so much owed by so many to so few.' Churchill's famous line sums up the magnitude of the importance of the victory in the 'Battle of Britain'. His words refer to the courage and sacrifice, in the face of overwhelming physical dangers, of the aircrews of the Royal Air Force who battled throughout the 'Spitfire summer' of 1940 to save Britain from German invasion.

Yet, while these men were at the apex of the battle with the Luftwaffe, many others contributed to Britain's triumph at this crucial stage of the war. Those manning coastal and inland defence guns and barrage balloons also helped protect the RAF aerodromes and the means of further aircraft production. While out at sea, merchant and royal navy ships ensured that imported resources got through to keep aircraft manufacturers, the country and its people supplied.

After the 'phoney war' between the beginning of the war on 3 September 1939 and April 1940, the Germans made rapid attacks on a number of European countries. This blitzkrieg, or 'lightning war', pushed British troops out of Europe, ending with the rescue of more than 330,000 men from the beaches of Dunkirk at the end of May and the first three days of June 1940. With Europe secure, Hitler's plan, codenamed Operation Sealion, was to invade Britain. In order to do this, he had to defeat the RAF whose aircraft would be able to attack the troop barges with which he planned to land his attacking forces.

So began the 'Battle of Britain'. Hitler had set the date of the 15 September as 'der tag', 'the day' which would herald the invasion of Britain. The hot summer of 1940 saw the development of new tactics of aerial warfare; civilians, particularly in the south-east corner of England, witnessed dogfights between Luftwaffe and RAF pilots as they fought for air superiority.

The day set for the invasion saw one of the fiercest air battles of the war in which the RAF lost twenty-seven aircraft to the Luftwaffe's fifty-six; by the end of the bigger battle the score was: RAF, 915; Luftwaffe, 1733. These figures highlight the numbers of airmen, on both sides, who died during these encounters; many of the first to lose their lives were the most experienced fliers and leaders either side possessed. For the RAF, those that survived became essential personnel in the battles to come: defending British cities against the nightly Blitz; flying bombing raids across enemy territory; pioneers in what was to become an essential tool of modern warfare.

This book is illustrated with dramatic photographs from the archives of the *Daily Mail*, many unseen since they were first taken and restored to original quality. The images have been selected to afford a sketch of Britain during those crucial few months, when liberty hung in the balance: hung in the hands of men and women who operated ground defences; hung, ultimately high in the sky, in the skills of young men prepared to risk their lives thousands of feet above Britain.

Summer of their finest hour

As with many of the most memorable phrases of the Second World War, the 'Battle of Britain' was a term coined by Winston Churchill in a speech to parliament on 17 June 1940. The speech was both an attempt to justify the policy of pursuing the war, and an attempt to bolster the morale of a nation which had in actuality been defeated in the battle to keep Europe free from Nazi occupation. Despite the skilful turning of the retreat from Dunkirk into a triumph of British spirit, and it was in many ways a triumph when 338,226 men were rescued, Britain faced a bleak and uncertain future. In his speech Churchill, only in office as Prime Minister for two months, spoke passionately about the task ahead:

The Battle of Britain is about to begin…The whole fury and might of the enemy must very soon be turned upon us. Hitler knows that he will have to break us in this island or lose the war. If we can stand up to him, all Europe may be free, and the life of the world may move forward into broad, sunlit uplands. But if we fail, the whole world, including the United States, including all that we have known and care for, will sink into the abyss of a new Dark Age, made more sinister by the lights of a perverted science. Let us therefore brace ourselves to our duties, and so bear ourselves that if the British Empire and its Commonwealth last for a thousand years, men will still say, "This was their finest hour."

Churchill's 'very soon' turned out to be a matter of weeks. The 10 July 1940 is officially nominated as the beginning of the Battle of Britain. Since the fall of France and the Dunkirk evacuation, the Luftwaffe had been carrying out raids on Britain, but with only half an hour's flying time over the country, they were limited in their range. On the first day there were raids on Swansea and Falmouth, as well as attacks on shipping convoys in the Bristol and English Channels which seemed, in magnitude, greater than anything seen in the previous weeks. British fighter aircraft were heavily outnumbered but managed to drive off the raiders.

Indeed at the start of the Battle, the Luftwaffe with 2,800 aircraft stationed in France, Belgium, Holland and Norway, outnumbered the RAF by four to one. Germany, having fought in the Spanish Civil War, had more combat-experienced pilots and, in the Messerschmitt 109, a superb fighter plane. Although fewer in number, RAF Fighter Command, under the leadership of Air Chief Marshall Sir Hugh Dowding, were well-served with the Hawker Hurricane and the Supermarine Spitfire. British fliers also had the advantage of being closer to their airfields and battling over their own territory. If they had to bale out or land a damaged plane, the flier and the machine could usually be restored to operational fitness; German pilots and planes downed over Britain were lost to Luftwaffe Command.

Between July and mid-August the 'battle' turned out to be a series of deadly aerial skirmishes above the skies of southern Britain. The RAF's losses in this period were tremendous; it seemed at some points that, statistically, the RAF would be annihilated, running out of aircraft faster than they could be replaced – to say nothing of the men involved. British fighter tactical training was based on experiences in the First World War. Despite official resistance to change, quite quickly RAF pilots learned that they had to amend a number of strategies, adopting some of those used by the Luftwaffe, such as flying pairs and fours, and changing the alignment of their machine guns. Regulation alignments in which the fighter's eight guns converged at 650 yards proved largely ineffectual against German bombers. It was necessary for a Hurricane or Spitfire to get closer and so convergence at 250 yards was more useful.

On 12 August, German tactics changed. At the beginning of the month, Hitler had given permission for an all out air attack on Britain, targeting airfields as well as the planes in the air. Bad weather and poor preparation meant that it was nearly two weeks before the attack, named 'Alderangriff' or Eagle attack, could be attempted. During the first few weeks of the battle there had been a growing realisation on the part of the German High Command of the importance of Britain's chain of stations housing Radio Direction Finding equipment (RDF or Radar). However, they underestimated its strength and flexibility and, despite an attempt to knock holes in the RDF chain just prior to the Eagle attack on 13 August, only one station, at Ventnor, was off the air for the attack.

Eagle attack on 13 August witnessed the greatest air battle of the war to date. The day started in confusion for the Germans with Luftwaffe commander Goering's orders to cancel the attack not reaching all aircrews, so that some early sorties were flown. Improving weather later saw the attack formally reinstated and part of the plan was to hit RAF airfields. Stuka bombers attacked several airfields, including an attack on Detling that killed sixty-seven airmen and destroyed twenty-two aircraft on the ground. However, Detling was not a Fighter Command airfield, a fact that points up the poor quality of much of Luftwaffe intelligence.

In 1940, Britain's intelligence was also not of the highest quality, but the Enigma machine codes had been broken by that time giving Fighter Command warning of the build up to attacks, if not details. On Eagle Day what was more important, as early warning of incoming enemy aircraft, was the information from the RDF chain, and the eyes the individuals of the Observer Corps, a volunteer service linked to Fighter Command. Discounting the planes lost on the ground, the attack on 13 August saw the RAF lose thirteen aircraft but bring down thirty-four.

Air battles like those witness on Eagle Day demanded much of the fighter pilots who flew to defend against the Luftwaffe attackers. As head of Fighter Command, Dowding had taken the decision to husband his resources, and use only the squadrons in south-east England, chiefly those in Number 11 Group, to engage the enemy. This put immense pressure on those squadrons. During a battle a fighter aircraft would typically have thirty-five minutes between sorties, when indefatigable ground crew would check the plane over, refuel and ready it for take-off, while the pilot was rested and debriefed.

Dowding's tactics were severely criticised, especially by Air Vice-Marshall Trafford Leigh-Mallory, head of Number 12 Group, the Command area adjacent to Number 11 Group lead by Keith Park, who also came in for criticism. Leigh-Mallory, together with the famous air ace, Douglas Bader, favoured 'big wings' tactics which suggested RAF fighters be sent to meet the Luftwaffe in equal numbers, engaging them before they reached Britain. Churchill heard of the criticisms and he began to lose faith in Dowding who was removed from command on 25 November 1940.

Arguments continue about the efficacy of Dowding's strategy, but he and Fighter Command did win out in the end. In this he was aided by poor decisions on the part of Reichmarschall Goering and the German High Command. Following on from the events of Eagle Day and further RAF victories in the following days, Goering chose to switch tactics, gambling on a battle of attrition. Daily, the Luftwaffe Messerschmitts would engage RAF Hurricanes and Spitfires, while Junkers Stuka and Dornier bombers would attempt to break through to attack the airfields. At night the Germans also attacked British towns responsible for aircraft production. All of this was intended to wear down both Fighter Command and the ground defences.

Even at night, when it disturbed their sleep, the booming sound of the anti-aircraft (ack-ack) guns was reassuring to British civilians. In fact at night ground defences were especially important. During the battle of Britain, the majority of Fighter Command's aircraft was not equipped to deal with enemy aircraft at night. Only a few Blenheims, and later the Beaufighter, had onboard Radar (RDF) equipment, but it was not particularly accurate against Luftwaffe planes which, fitted with radio beam targeting equipment, the 'knickebein', were able to

The switch to night bombing of cities and fewer daytime raids, gave Fighter Command sufficient respite to recoup and regroup ready for what is seen as the decisive battle in the Battle of Britain. Under Lord Beaverbrook, who had been given charge of the newly-formed Ministry of Aircraft Production when Churchill became Prime Minister, British fighter aircraft production doubled. By September 1940 the aircraft industry was turning out around a hundred and twenty fighter planes each week. New aircraft, together with the sterling work done by ground crews to repair and bring back into service damaged machines, and the rest given to combat-fatigued pilots, gave Dowding a force with which to meet the last great assault.

On 15 September, the Luftwaffe attacked in huge formation. This was the day that had originally been set as the date for the German invasion of Britain, so it had immense significance for Hitler and Goering. Although the final tally of twenty-seven losses for Fighter Command to fifty-six downed Luftwaffe aircraft was not a particularly remarkable score, the fact that the RAF was able to mount such a massive force was of momentous consequence. The Germans felt beaten and, together with the deteriorating autumn weather, an invasion seemed no longer feasible. Two days later, on 17 September, Hitler postponed indefinitely 'Operation Sealion', as the invasion plans had been codenamed. Never again did the Luftwaffe come in such numbers to engage Fighter Command and by the end of October the Battle of Britain was deemed to be over.

bomb at night with great accuracy. British scientists engineered a system to jam the transmissions and by September 1940 the knickebein had been overcome. A similar fate befell the 'X-Gerat' beam developed by Germany as a replacement.

These issues came to the fore at the beginning of September when Germany altered strategy once again. Working on poor intelligence and in some respects the thought of revenge for a bombing raid on Berlin, Hitler and Goering order an all-out attack on London. On 7 September, the Blitz began with a massive raid targeting the capital's docks which were set ablaze, killing or injuring around two thousand people. The attack on London, ironically, bought time for Fighter Command which, with the attrition tactics of the previous few weeks, was seriously compromised and nearing the limits of its machinery and manpower. However, the Germans believed that their policy was not working, never guessing how serious Dowding's situation was.

Despite the RAF's victory in the Battle of Britain, the war with Germany was not ended and there was much to be done by the aircrews that had been the heroes of the summer of 1940. They had 'held the fort' while the army, suffering loss of men and equipment after the fall of France, began to regroup and rearm. But Britain was not yet ready to mount an attack against Germany and for the next few months Fighter Command had an essential, if less prominent role, in Britain's air defences as they flew out to engage Luftwaffe fighter aircraft and bombers as they attempted to destroy the means of munitions production and British morale. The very morale that the skills and courage of the aircrews of Fighter Command had bolstered throughout the Battle of Britain by their incredible ability to survive in the face of overwhelming dangers, a reflection of the position the nation found itself facing.

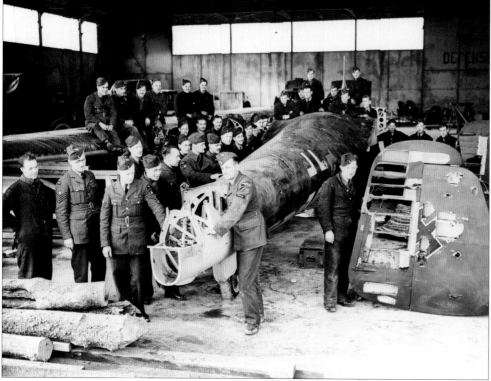

The Western Front

Opposite page: In 1939 and early 1940 the RAF had a role with the British Expeditionary Force (BEF) which was fighting in France. The force flew reconnaissance missions and protected troops against attack from Luftwaffe fighters. This spectacular photograph is taken from the rear of a Hurricane flying in formation over France in April 1940 - the planes are just breaking formation and are about to engage with enemy aircraft.

Above: A squadron of RAF fighters flies into the dawn as it sets off on a reconnaissance mission in November 1939.

Left: RAF men group around a captured Luftwaffe Dornier where it is set out for expert examination in a shed in France.

Camouflage

Right: Under this odd tent lies an aircraft (note the propeller at the front) which can be airborne in seconds. This plane is stationed in France where it was clearly necessary to hide from enemy surveillance. Even in Britain, aircraft were sometimes camouflaged on the ground or dummy planes stored on aerodromes to misinform the Luftwaffe of the RAF's strength.

Above: This group of pilots were some of the men responsible for bringing down fifteen enemy aircraft in two days when they were first stationed in France during May 1940 as Britain fought alongside the Free French to try to avoid the fall of France.

Opposite above: After receiving a direct hit from anti-aircraft guns over Norway just days before Britain withdrew its forces in May 1940, this Lockheed Hudson was piloted safely back to Britain with her crew all unhurt.

Opposite below: Vapour trails in the sky signal to those on the ground that fighter aircraft are in action.

Operation Dynamo

By the end of May 1940 the British
Expeditionary Force had been driven back to
the coast in north-east France. There was little
hope of escape but Winston Churchill, who
had recently taken over as Prime Minister
oversaw a daring plan, codenamed Operation
Dynamo, to rescue the British troops from the
beaches. Thousands of seaworthy vessels in
Britain, from Channel ferries to fishing boats,
private yachts to sailing dinghies, crossed the
Channel to bring the men home. It was
estimated that fewer than 50,000 could be
rescued; in the event 338,226 were saved. The
RAF played an important role in protecting the
troops on the beach from attack by Luftwaffe
planes.

Below and opposite below: The men wait
patiently and in an orderly fashion for their turn
to be rescued.

Right: Troops wade out to a ship waiting to
rescue them.

Opposite above: A ship, laden with rescued
troops, sets off for home as Dunkirk burns in
the background.

Back to Britain – in pyjamas!

Opposite page: These two soldiers arrived back in Britain wearing pyjamas and, like many of their comrades, had few belongings and little equipment with them. The necessity for a quick evacuation from Dunkirk meant that much was left behind - the priority was the men.

Above: Disembarking at an English port on 31 May 1940; the faces of these troops of the British Expeditionary Force show their relief at being back on British soil.

Left: Some of the equipment rescued from Dunkirk. But while this photograph was published, reassuring the country that all was not lost, in truth the stock of weaponry was seriously depleted as much was left behind in France. The RAF had lost the equivalent of three squadrons' worth of planes. Despite these losses, the retreat from Dunkirk was turned from disaster to triumph by the unimagined success of Operation Dynamo in rescuing the vast majority of the British Force.

Welcome home, boys

Left and above left: Women and children greet the men on their return from the beaches of Dunkirk, offering food and a handshake. After landing at British ports, trains took the troops to their barracks. As they arrived at stations throughout the country they were given a hero's welcome.

Above right: A pie and a cup of tea are suitable welcome home gifts for these two. Many men had to wait for hours or days on the beaches for rescue, supported only by whatever rations they had themselves.

Opposite: The story accompanying this picture tells of how the soldier holding the gun, a Belgian automatic pistol, used the weapon when his own ammunition ran out. While the tale was told in a jovial way it highlights the difficulties the British Expeditionary Force found itself in when the Germans attacked and cut supply lines.

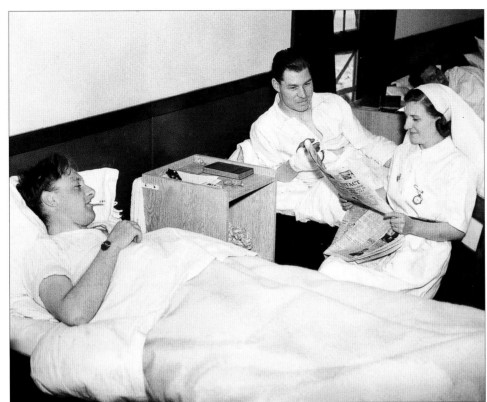

Exhausted and injured

Left: A ward sister reads to two men of the Royal Artillery in a northern hospital as they recover from injuries sustained as they fought against the German blitzkrieg through Belgium and France.

Below: Wounded soldiers, rescued from the beaches at Dunkirk, rest and take the air in a hospital in Hertfordshire.

Opposite above: Exhausted men, who had been fighting day and night for three weeks before they were evacuated from Dunkirk, take the opportunity to doze at a reception centre before their leave begins.

Opposite below: Weary troops disembark at a British port - their faces strained and their comradeship evident.

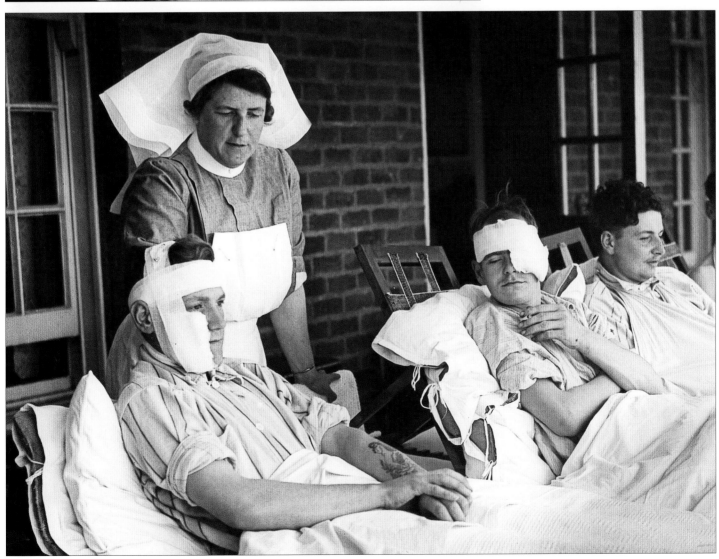

'Their finest hour'

Opposite page: Winston Churchill, pictured here trying on a flying helmet (*above left*) and inspecting coastal defences, had become Prime Minister on 11 May 1940, following the resignation of Neville Chamberlain, whom Parliament had deemed too weak to deal with the German blitzkrieg in Europe. On assuming office he had to face the humiliation of a withdrawal from Europe and the realisation that Britain and its Commonwealth would be left to fight Germany alone. On 17 June he broadcast to the nation that the Battle of Britain was about to begin and that in the country's future people would say that 'this was their finest hour'.

Left: Two of the sailors involved with rescuing troops from Dunkirk head off on leave.

Below: Some of the small ships that were part of the 'armada' that helped in the evacuation of Dunkirk are pictured heading up the Thames, returning to their berths.

Barrage defences

Above left and right: WAAFs raising a barrage balloon. Barrage balloons were an important form of defence against enemy aircraft. When information was passed to a barrage balloon site that enemy planes had been sighted, the balloons, which were normally tethered close to the ground, were raised as a deterrent to low-flying aircraft. Without the ability to come in low over the target, the accuracy of a bombing run was compromised. Initially it was thought that women would not be able manage the heavy work of raising and lowering the balloons but eventually they became essential personnel on many barrage balloon sites.

Right: As these women pull on guy-ropes to lower the balloon, the effort required is evident.

Opposite page: A WAAF checks that the balloon is securely tethered.

Roof spotters

Above left: Most work places and institutions employed 'roof spotters' whose task it was to watch on the roof of the building for enemy aircraft and to send a warning to colleagues to seek shelter in case of attack. Pictured here are spotters on the roof of the American Embassy.

Above right: Two members of the Girl Guide Association watch the skies for signs of enemy planes on the roof of their association's headquarters in London.

Right: Spotters on the roof of the *Daily Mail*'s Northcliffe House follow the vapour trails in a battle between RAF and Luftwaffe fighters thousands of feet above London.

Opposite above: A giant map in the operations room of Coastal Command records the position of British and enemy ships and submarines.

Opposite below: These members of a barrage balloon crew at Dover are credited with bringing down a Messerschmitt during an attack on their balloon.

The eyes of Britain's air defences

Above: An Observer Corps control room which received reports from outlying observation posts. Information then passed to regional centres in direct touch with Fighter Command.

Left: Mr Watkins, a famous Welsh tenor, stands ready to transmit details to the control centre as architect, Mr Peter Pointon Taylor, scans the sky for signs of enemy aircraft. Observers volunteered their free time to help the country's defences.

Opposite above: Using range and direction finding equipment an Observer Corps party watch the skies around London.

Opposite below: ATS learn how to use the equipment at an anti-aircraft battery.

Ack-ack gunners

Above: One of the first Auxiliary Territorial Service (ATS) women to be trained to use the targeting instruments on anti-aircraft guns. Women were not allowed to handle the actual guns but, from spring 1940, mixed anti-aircraft, or 'ack-ack', batteries became quite common.

Right: Loading a shell into a gun at this London anti-aircraft unit.

Opposite above: A group of Welsh gunners rush to their station on the evening of 29 August 1940, during a crucial period of the Battle of Britain when the Luftwaffe attacked in force.

Opposite below: A crew in action. While the majority of German planes were downed by fighter planes, the AA gunners played an important role. They could break up a formation of bombers, disable enemy aircraft and hamper their bombing accuracy.

Searching the skies

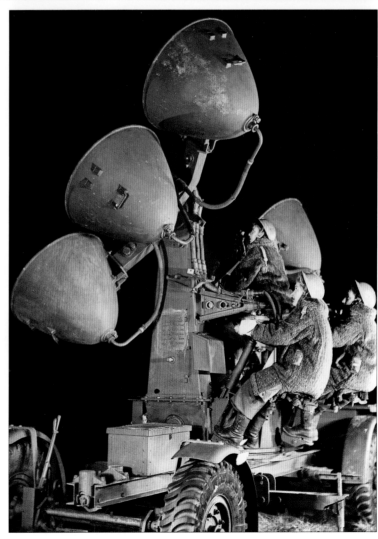

Right: This unusual contraption is a device which attempted to locate night-flying enemy aircraft by sound. Searchlights were a far more effective way of locating and tracking aircraft. Of course the problem with searchlights was that they gave the Luftwaffe bombers a clear target, so they had to be used judiciously, only being switched on to track specific planes.

Above and opposite below: With their guns pointed to the skies, the image and the idea of the anti-aircraft battery was a comforting one to the British public. Even though the noise might have been annoying, it was also reassuring to civilians to know that they were being protected as they went about their daily lives, or slept in their shelters. During the Battle of Britain, the gunners were credited, sometimes at the expense of Fighter Command, with more downed aircraft than they had achieved; an important strategy to maintain public morale.

Opposite above: In late September 1940, an officer checks the ammunition while in the background the gun is cleaned. At this stage of the battle the guns were in almost constant nightly use. As a desperate response to the heavy night bombing raids, particularly on London, General Frederick Pile, commander-in-chief of AA Command, ordered a 'barrage' of shells against the bombers. It was an inefficient strategy. The 260,000 rounds of heavy ammunition fired brought down only a relatively small number of German aircraft, but it did hinder bombing accuracy and made the blitzed citizens feel safer.

Bomb damage

Above: The effects of a bombing raid on a row of south-east houses in the early hours of the morning of 15 July 1940. Later on in the Battle of Britain, civilians would find themselves increasingly under attack when the German High Command decided to target them in an attempt to demoralise so that the British government would be pressed to surrender. The first major attack was on London on 7 September 1940, marking the beginning of the Blitz which was to last until May 1941.

Left: A farm labourer in Kent holds the remains of an incendiary bomb found in the village of Chilham in May 1940.

Opposite above: A huge crater from a bomb dropped by a Junkers bomber during the massive air battle that took place on 15 August 1940. The plane was later brought down nearby.

Opposite below: In a wood near Canterbury a man stands in the crater left by a high-explosive bomb. This corner of the south-east was known as 'Hellfire Corner' because, as the closest part of Britain to continental Europe, it suffered frequent bombing.

Churchill visits 'Hellfire Corner'

Above: Winston Churchill chats to soldiers during a visit to Ramsgate on a tour to see the damage done by German raids on 'Hellfire Corner', the area of the south-east coast which suffered most from German bombing during the summer of 1940. During his visit there was an almost continual alert but he carried on unperturbed. At this stage of the Battle of Britain, the end of August 1940, the Luftwaffe had stepped up the attack in an attempt to grind down the RAF's resistance.

Opposite above: A German plane plummets to the ground after an air battle with Spitfires over the Sussex Downs in the third week of August 1940.

Opposite below: In October 1940, women and their babies, evacuated from the dangers of the Blitz on London, shelter in a roadside ditch as a Luftwaffe plane strafes the ground with machine-gun fire.

Action stations

Above: Aircraft lined up on the runway, ready to go if the call comes for them to step into action. These are new planes, presented to the Air Ministry by the East India Fund, but once they had flown even one mission the process of repair and maintenance began.

Left: Men from the West Lancashire RAF Squadron (and their dog, Joker!) rush to their aircraft as they receive the call 'action stations'.

Opposite above: Although they look as if they are taking part in a fun run these pilots are answering a call for reinforcements during an air battle over the south-east on 1 September 1940.

Opposite below: Fighter pilots run to their planes during an alert. All signals to scramble came from Fighter Command HQ at Bentley Priory where information from RDF (Radar) stations or the Observer Corps was received.

The ones that did not get away

Opposite: Residents of Kent examine part of the wreckage of a German plane that landed in their gardens. The aircraft had been shot down during a raid in August 1940.

Right: A pall of black smoke rises from the flames engulfing the wreckage of this Luftwaffe aircraft, downed as it headed home over the south-east coast.

Below left: While this aircraft's machine gun lies intact on the ground, the remainder of the plane lies as wreckage strewn across the field.

Below right: It takes two men to try to remove the propeller from this plane shot down in the Thames Estuary area. The south-east corner of England saw the greatest action during the 'Spitfire Summer' of 1940 as it was the closest area to Luftwaffe bases in Germany and continental Europe. Additionally, the development of radar meant that the RAF was able to intercept raiders soon after they crossed the Channel.

Fighters in action

Opposite above: Smoke trails from the Messerschmitt as the Spitfire chases its prey.

Opposite below: In the top right of the picture a Hurricane makes a victory sweep above the burning wreckage of a Heinkel 111 which was caught by the RAF fighter as it returned home after a bombing raid on London in September 1940.

Above: A fighter squadron flies into action on 29 July 1940 when the Luftwaffe attacked 'Hellfire Corner' and shipping in the Channel.

Left: An armed guard stands sentry over the wreckage of a Dornier bomber which had been shot down before penetrating London's air defences.

Luftwaffe wreckage

Opposite above: Brought down on 2 September 1940, this Messerschmitt was part of a formation protecting bombers. Late August and early September was a critical period in the Battle of Britain. RAF bases were subject to relentless attacks and, as many that summer witnessed, it was the skill of the British fighter pilots that frequently turned the raiders back.

Opposite below: Airmen show off the markings on this Spitfire chalking up the downing of two Luftwaffe bombers.

Above top: Two German planes lie wrecked on the beach on the south-east coast.

Above: A Junkers 88 which made a forced landing is examined by mechanics.

Left: A distant fire in the Surrey hills marks the position of an aircraft shot down at the start of a raid on London.

Shot down!

Below: A remarkable picture of an aerial attack on a Heinkel, taken by a camera-gun synchronised with the machine guns on board the Hurricane fighter that shot the German plane down.

Left: A marine mine-laying plane loaded with munitions crashed at Clacton on 30 April 1940. It destroyed several houses. The aircraft's task was to lay anti-shipping mines in the North Sea. The incident brought home to the British public the dangers of bomb-laden planes falling in built-up areas.

Opposite above: RAF salvage men at a scrap heap where the wrecks of German aircraft were stored. Scrap materials from Luftwaffe planes were recycled in RAF machines and these two large wrecks are being transported to a 'Spitfire Fund' exhibition.

Opposite below: A cow grazes peacefully among the wreckage of a bomber downed in August 1940.

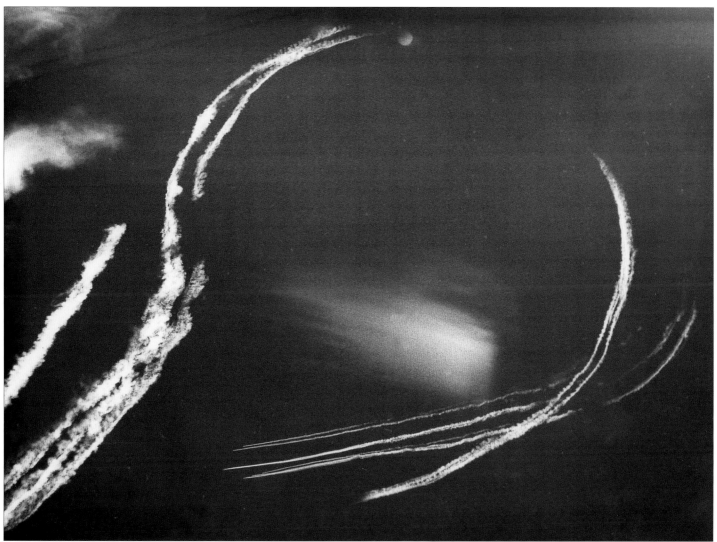

Conquering the raiders

Opposite above: British anti-aircraft shells burst around a formation of 23 German planes on 19 August 1940. The accompanying caption suggests that 13 of the aircraft were shot down and the rest turned tail without reaching their objective.

Opposite below: A spectacular image, taken with a camera-gun synchronised with the machine guns on a Spitfire captures the moment this Dornier plummets to the ground.

Above: The vapour trails of the aircraft mark the moment they dive into the fight.

Right: In a Surrey cemetery lie the graves of German airmen killed on 'Eagle Day', 13 August 1940.

Messerschmitt 109 on show at Windsor

Left: On display in the castle grounds, a Messerschmitt 109 (Me 109) that crashed in Windsor Great Park at the height of the Battle of Britain.

Above: Soldiers stand guard over a Junkers 88 bomber brought down by RAF fighters on 13 August 1940 (Eagle Day). On that day, following a massive but ill-coordinated attack, the Luftwaffe lost 34 aircraft to the RAF's 13, although several German bombers had managed to evade defences and drop their load on British airfields.

Opposite above left: For the cost of 6d you could examine this Me 110, the latest German fighter-bomber, which had been brought down in Kent.

Opposite above right: RAF men inspect the 'little devil' design painted onto the cowling of a wrecked Messerschmitt.

Opposite below: The tailplane of this Me 109 sports a tally of the 'kills' the pilot had made before he was brought down by British air defences.

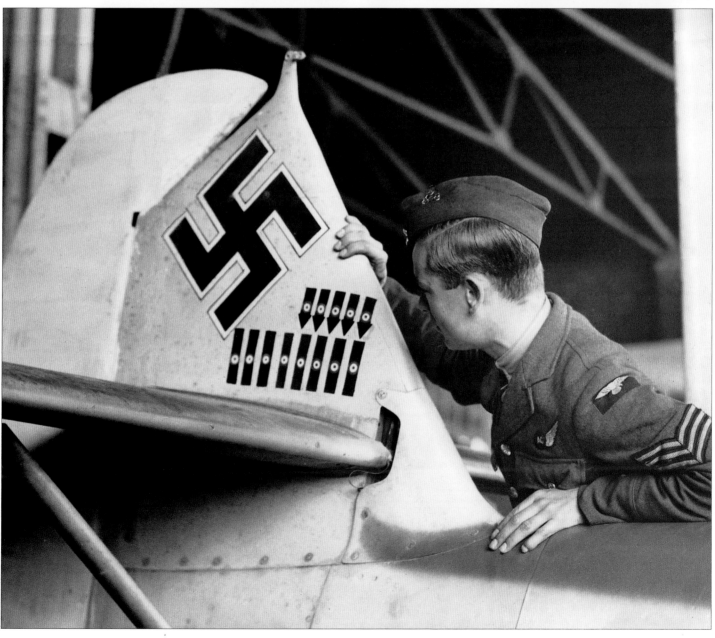

Time for lunch?

Opposite page: Two workmen stop to eat their lunch in the cockpit of this Luftwaffe plane. They are stripping out the parts from the aircraft for re-use in British machines.

Right: A salvage worker retrieves a machine gun from one of five planes shot down on the south coast on 'Eagle Day', 13 August 1940. On that day the Germans' aim was to deal a deadly blow to the RAF. In the event the attack was postponed because of poor weather but the delaying order failed to reach all commanders and some bomber crews attacked Britain. While the Luftwaffe lost 34 aircraft, they did manage to hit several airfields.

Below: Breaking up the fuselage of a Luftwaffe plane, ready for the parts to be transported for re-use.

Rescued – but he got his man

Above and left: Rescued from the Channel in late August 1940, when he had to bale out after downing a German bomber, this Spitfire pilot is welcomed ashore. At this stage of the battle, between 24 August and 6 September, the German tactics changed in an all-out attempt to destroy British Fighter Command. Massive attacks on airfields and on other strategic targets during the day forced the British into committing large numbers of fighters. The Luftwaffe followed up with night-time bombing of aircraft production sites.

Opposite page: A captured Heinkel 111 bomber looks threatening from this angle.

Flying in formation

Right: One of the most well known of fighter aircraft and the fastest machine the RAF had at its disposal, a Supermarine Spitfire is put through its paces.

Opposite page: An echelon of Hawker Hurricane aircraft in flight (*above*) and (*below*) a single aircraft. Hurricanes formed the backbone of the RAF's fighter strength during the Battle of Britain. Despite the fact that they would appear to have been outclassed by the Me 109, the RAF's 1,715 Hurricanes were responsible for over three-quarters of the Luftwaffe planes taken out of action by Fighter Command.

Below: One of the Hurricanes in this formation took part in a test flight from Edinburgh to London, covering the distance in 48 minutes.

Hitting the target

Opposite page: The wreckage of two barrage balloons plummets to the ground after being shot by Messerschmitt 109s on 1 September 1940. One of the Luftwaffe aircraft was brought down by rifle fire from the balloon crew.

Above: Two Dornier aircraft, photographed from above by another German plane, fly over the target during the Battle of Britain.

Right: An Me 109 attacks a barrage balloon protecting the Kent coast in late August 1940, a time when the Luftwaffe had stepped up their attacks in a war of attrition.

Night fighters

Above: Crew from a night fighter squadron get a last-minute weather forecast. A few Blenheim aircraft, and later the Beaufighter, were equipped with radar which helped track and locate Luftwaffe bombers in the dark. However, the RAF had much less success at interception at night than during the day; the Blenheims in particular were not as mobile as Hurricanes and Spitfires.

Left: Pilots, in their leather flying jackets, study maps of the area they will patrol during the night.

Opposite above left: A Spitfire pilot shows the small (red) button on the column which he has to press to fire all eight of his aircraft's machine guns.

Opposite above right: An intelligence officer records the pilot's observations as he reports on a sortie just flown.

Opposite below: In a moment of calm observers on a night patrol plot their course with one of the pilots who looks on from his perch on the back of the sofa.

'Ginger' Lacey

James 'Ginger' Lacey was the RAF ace who, with a tally of 18, brought down more German aircraft than anyone else during the Battle of Britain. He survived the war and had to relearn how to fly in 1973 as he had allowed his flying licence to lapse. He died in Yorkshire in May 1989 at the age of 72.

Left: In July 1940 'Ginger' Lacey was awarded a parachute and a scarf in recognition of his actions in bringing down a Heinkel which had bombed Buckingham Palace. Here he receives the parachute.

Below: The scarf bearing the names of the workers in Australia who made the parachute is displayed.

Opposite page: Flight-Lieutenant Lacey wears the parachute and scarf made specially for him.

Douglas Bader

Opposite page: One of the RAF's most famous and skilled fliers, Douglas Bader had to battle to win a place in the service he had been forced to leave after he lost both his legs in an air crash in 1931. Reinstalled as a pilot, he flew throughout the Battle of Britain, his artificial legs proving to be no handicap.

Below: Squadron Leader Bader pictured just after being awarded the DSO with, to his right, Pilot Officer W. L. Knight and, on his left, Flight Lieutenant G. E. Ball, both awarded DFC.

Right: Squadron Leader R. R. Stanford-Tuck has his tally of hits on German aircraft recorded on his fuselage.

Young heroes

This page: New Zealand-born pilot 'Al' Deere had one of the most hectic war careers. He saw service throughout the war, downing 17 German aircraft during the Battle of Britain. He had to bale out of his own machine on numerous occasions.

Opposite above left: A pilot with a picture of Mae West on his 'Mae West', the life jacket worn by aircrew over their uniforms.

Opposite above right: Portrait of a nameless pilot, taken to show the 'breed of men who pilot the Spitfires'.

Opposite below left: Wing Commander Brian Kingcombe, who flew as a flight lieutenant with 92 Squadron was awarded the DFC and the DSO for his service with the RAF. He survived the war and died in February 1994.

Opposite below right: Pilot Officer Richard Hillary flew with 603 Squadron. He wrote his autobiography before his death in action in 1943.

Fighter pilot glamour

Right: Squadron Leader Anthony Bartley with his fiancee, Deborah Kerr, a Hollywood film star. The squadron leader, who claimed eight 'kills' during the Battle of Britain, epitomised the image of the attractive, glamorous young RAF pilot.

Below and opposite above right: These three portraits were part of a series taken in October 1940 to celebrate the RAF pilots who risked their lives in defence of the country. The accompanying caption to the pictures reads: 'The admiration of the world has been held by the brilliant exploits of Britain's Spitfire pilots. Their daring and accuracy, and the superior design of eight-gun Spitfires, have proved the deadliest foe of enemy aircraft, and Britain's surest defence.'

Opposite above left: A smiling pilot, pictured on return from a sortie at the end of July 1940 which involved an aerial battle above the Channel.

Opposite below: Even before the Battle of Britain commenced newspapers made much of the individual pilot's experiences. This pilot was reported in April 1940 for his courage, quick wits and skill in engaging and downing a Dornier on the Western Front.

601 Squadron

Above: The men of 601 Squadron (City of London) pictured at the end of the Battle of Britain. The caption to this picture claims the squadron had destroyed 'more than 100 enemy aircraft' and that ten of the pilots had been awarded the DFC. The squadron was sometimes nicknamed 'the millionaire squadron' as it was principally composed of wealthy young men, including an American named Billy Fiske who joined the unit in 1940. He died in August of that same year following a crash-landing of his Hurricane.

Left: On a tour of RAF Fighter Stations, King George shakes hands with members of a squadron about to go off on patrol.

Opposite above: The King, on the same tour, awards decorations to RAF aircrew.

Opposite below: Pilots pictured on return from a daylight sweep over German-occupied France. Each of the pilots had been decorated for his service.

A break from the battle

Left: A squadron leader grabs a cup of tea and a chat with a New Zealand pilot during a break from the battle on 15 August 1940. This day saw one of the biggest and most ferocious air battles of the war. Germany lost more than 56 aircraft to the RAF's 27.

Below: Airmen relax at Biggin Hill aerodrome on 31 August 1940. At this stage of the Battle of Britain the RAF were flying numerous missions as Luftwaffe Command attempted to put airfields out of action. Biggin Hill did in fact suffer a degree of damage.

Opposite above: Aircrew in the steel helmets which were required headgear during an alert. Leather flying helmets would be donned as soon as they got the signal to take to the air.

Opposite below right: A Biggin Hill fighter pilot shows off a souvenir bullet hole in his flying helmet. The 'injury' was sustained during an aerial battle over Dover on 29 July 1940.

Opposite below left: 'The confident smiles of this group of Spitfire Pilots gives evidence of the fine type of man who is daily engaging the enemy airman.'

Waiting for the call

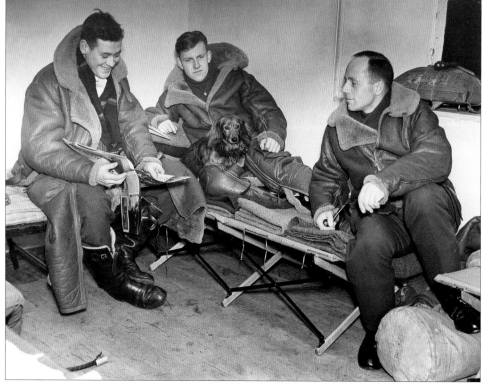

Above: An RAF coastal patrol rest in their hut but are always ready to take off on an emergency operational flight.

Left: All the creature comforts in this night fighter squadron's rest room!

Opposite above: 'These men don't suffer from "cold feet"' reads the caption to this picture of a fighter station that by the end of 1940 claimed 600 Luftwaffe 'scalps'.

Opposite below: The life of a pilot was unpredictable, sometimes flying a continual series of sorties, sometimes just waiting around for the next call. At the height of the Battle of Britain, fliers were often exhausted and had to snatch a sleep whenever and wherever they could.

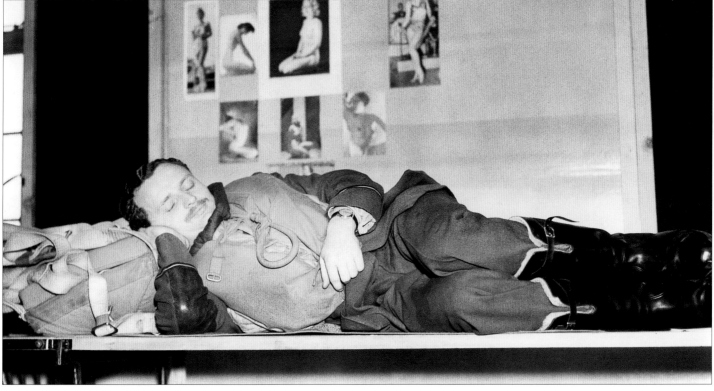

Civilian pilots

Left: Pilots from the National Air Communications Pool at an aerodrome 'somewhere in the west country'. These pilots are not members of the military but were employed, along with their civilian aircraft, once owned by Imperial and British Airways, by the Air Ministry. Like RAF pilots, they had to be ready to take off at a moment's notice to transport whatever was required. While they were not intended to be involved in the fighting, over 200 non-combatant aircraft were shot down during the Battle of Britain.

Below: RAF pilots play shove ha'penny and prepare lime juice and soda as they await the call to scramble.

Opposite above: A rest in the sunshine for these two airmen.

Opposite below: Playing skittles in the mess is one way to get in some target practice!

Paying respects

Opposite above: A last salute is fired by his comrades at the funeral of Pilot Officer William (Billy) Fiske, an American who joined the 601 Squadron and lost his life after an air battle on 16 August 1940.

Opposite below: A gathering of 'the Few' still serving in the RAF prepare for their part in the funeral of Sir Winston Churchill in January 1965. They were led by Air Commodore Alan (Al) Deere (*far left*).

Above: A game of chess to pass the time in the pilots' rest room. Games, reading, listening to the radio or records on the gramophone, sleeping or chatting were all ways to pass the time while waiting for the call to action.

Right: Men at this fighter station salute King George after he has decorated officers and sergeants.

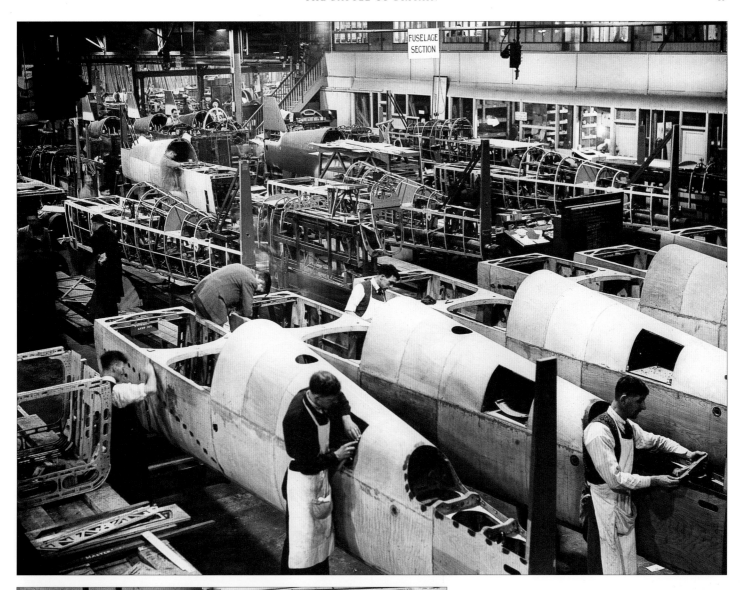

Hundreds of Hurricanes

Opposite page: Hurricane fighters in production at a factory in the east of England. Just before the Battle of Britain began the Ministry of Aircraft Production had been created with the newspaper tycoon, Lord Beaverbrook at its head. Beaverbrook set about dramatically increasing production, focusing on fighter aircraft rather than bombers. It was an inspired move as Hurricanes and Spitfires were just what was needed during the summer and autumn of 1940.

Above: Bodies for the Miles Master, an RAF training aircraft, in production.

Left: Bristol Beaufort bombers in the assembly shop in October 1940. It should be remembered that the aircrews of Bomber Command flew sorties deep into German territory throughout the Battle of Britain, attempting to destroy Luftwaffe planes on the ground and in production.

Spitfires capture the British imagination

Above: An impressive photograph of a Spitfire production line. Despite the fact that, throughout the Battle of Britain, the 1,715 Hurricanes that took part outnumbered the Spitfire by two to one and were responsible for more than three-quarters of the hits on enemy planes, it was the faster Spitfire, powered by a single Rolls-Royce engine, that captured the public imagination. The Hurricane was a reliable workhorse, robust enough to withstand shellbursts, while the Spitfire's speed and manoeuvrability was admired by the pilots and civilians alike.

Far left: Numerous 'Spitfire Funds' were set up around the country. Groups of people would fundraise to pay for a Spitfire. Here nineteen-year-old Nora Margaret Fish hands over a Spitfire named 'Counter Attack' to an RAF pilot in October 1940. NAAFI canteen workers had raised the money to pay for the machine.

Left: Funds raised from spectators who viewed this shot-down Messerschmitt went to the Croydon Spitfire Fund. The public were responsible for building aircraft, not only with their finances, but with donated metal, especially aluminium pots and pans which were melted and re-used to produce aircraft parts.

Convoys

Opposite above: The guns of an escort vessel protect a convoy of merchant ships as they make their way to port. In April 1940, when this photograph was taken, convoys had to run the gauntlet of German U-boats in the Atlantic. With the fall of France and the Battle of Britain they also became vulnerable to shelling from France and air attack.

Opposite below: August 1940 and this convoy is attacked by German gun batteries on the French coast. The picture was taken by *Daily Mail* photographer H. A. Wallace on board one of the escorting warships.

Above: A convoy of ships carrying food for rationed Britons makes its way along the east coast.

Left: 'Kipper Patrol' pilots who fly sorties to keep watch over sailors in the North Sea visit their 'charges' but need a lift ashore to their hosts' small fishing village.

Battle of Dover Straits

Opposite above: During the summer of 1940 the Channel was a scene of constant battle, both in the air and at sea. Here a convoy in the Straits of Dover is attacked by German aircraft. A bomb drops short of its target and an escorting destroyer fires anti-aircraft shells at the attackers.

Opposite below: Photographed from the cliffs at Dover, an attack from the French coast on a convoy in the Channel. It is the same attack pictured on page 87 from on board a ship in the Channel.

Above: The White Cliffs of Dover can be seen clearly behind the ship and the shellburst. The shell was fired from the French coast where German long-range guns could sometimes reach the town of Dover itself.

Left: Small barrage balloons, called kite balloons, being ferried to a convoy leaving port; the boats collect balloons from any inward bound ships using them. RAF personnel, stationed at all the major ports, maintained and repaired the equipment. Kite balloons were introduced after the Battle of Britain to try to prevent some of the attacks on shipping suffered at that time: dive-bombing by Junkers 87 Stuka dive-bombers or low flying swoops on ships' masts.

Royal Naval Patrol Service

Above: The men handling the anti-aircraft gun on board a naval training ship are members of the Royal Naval Patrol Service. They are fishermen who have joined this service to take part in minesweeping exercises at sea.

Right: With their guns ready for action these Royal Navy warships provide reassuring cover for convoys of merchant ships. Nevertheless, sailing aboard a merchant ship was just as dangerous as being aboard a military vessel. Merchant ships faced attack at sea from German U-boats, and closer to shore they could be attacked by the Luftwaffe or risk sailing into a mine.

Opposite page: Puffs of smoke in the sky mark the anti-aircraft shells bursting round the German planes which have just dropped their bombs. Fortunately the German munitions miss their mark and do no more than make the ships at sea bob about like corks in the backwash of the hundred-foot-high waterspout.

Fleet Air Arm

Left: Men of the Fleet Air Arm discuss plans around the stove in the Operations Room. The Fleet Air Arm is described as the 'winged infant of the Royal Navy' in the accompanying caption. It was an embryonic service. Although the navy had used aircraft in the First World War, it was not until 1937 that the Naval Air Branch, later the Fleet Air Arm, was set up. It was a child which grew quickly, from 232 aircraft deployed in 20 squadrons in 1939 to 3,700 planes, 59 aircraft carriers and 72,000 men by the end of the war.

Below: Naval ratings pictured at their training base at HMS *Kestrel* which was actually an aerodrome and not a ship, although German radio frequently reported it sunk!

Opposite page: A sailor signals to a merchant ship from a Royal Navy control base from where it is guided through the minefields that surround the coast.

Battle won but not the war

Left: By the end of October 1940, the Battle of Britain was over. The last major daylight attack was on 29 October. But, while the Battle of Britain might have been won, the war was not, and the RAF was called on to develop night fighter capability to defend British towns and cities against Luftwaffe night bombing raids, as well as to offer support to ground troops in the various theatres of war that opened up over the next five years. Pictured here is a formation of new Hurricane fighters, able to operate both by day and night, donated to the RAF by the people of the United Provinces of India.

Below: Refuelling Hurricane fighter aircraft. These planes consumed one motorist's yearly petrol allowance in just two hours of flying. The battle for civilians to conserve resources and in which merchant seamen risked their lives to import fuel had to continue beyond the Battle of Britain.

Opposite above right: Smoke from a downed Messerschmitt that had been escorting bombers on their way to attack London.

Opposite above left: Fortunately the plane fast approaching the tail of this British warplane is friendly; a cannon-firing Spitfire moves into position during a training exercise.

Opposite below: Hurricane fighters set off on patrol. Despite the existence of RDF, Radio Direction Finding, later Radar, patrols by RAF planes continued to be an important feature of Britain's air defences.

ACKNOWLEDGEMENTS

The photographs in this book are from the archives of the *Daily Mail*.
Particular thanks to Steve Torrington, Dave Sheppard, Brian Jackson,
Alan Pinnock, Paul Rossiter, Richard Jones and all the staff.

Thanks also to Cliff Salter, Richard Betts, John Dunne
Peter Wright, Trevor Bunting, Simon Taylor and Don Henry.

Design by Judy Linard.